Rough Cut
Thirty Years of Senryu

Rough Cut
Thirty Years of Senryu

WILLIAM SCOTT GALASSO

GALWIN PRESS

Rough Cut: Thirty Years of Senryu
Published by GALWIN PRESS
LAGUNA WOODS, CALIFORNIA

Copyright ©2019 WILLIAM SCOTT GALASSO.
All rights reserved.

No part of this book may be reproduced in any form or by any mechanical means, including information storage and retrieval systems without permission in writing from the publisher/author, except by a reviewer who may quote passages in a review.

All images, logos, quotes, and trademarks included in this book are subject to use according to trademark and copyright laws of the United States of America.

Library of Congress Control Number: 2019911392

GALASSO, WILLIAM SCOTT, Author
Rough Cut: Thirty Years of Senryu
WILLIAM SCOTT GALASSO

ISBN: **978-1-7327527-1-9**

POETRY / Relationships/Family/Humor
POETRY / Senryu

QUANTITY PURCHASES: Schools, companies, professional groups, clubs, and other organizations may qualify for special terms when ordering quantities of this title. For information, email galwinpress@yahoo.com.

All rights reserved by
WILLIAM SCOTT GALASSO and GALWIN PRESS.
This book is printed in the United States of America.

Additional Credits/Assistance:

Copyright ©2019

Cover Design: Deanna Estes
www.lotusdesign.biz

Consultant: Susie Schaefer, CPC
www.Finish the Book Publishing.com

Front Cover Portrait: Vicki Galasso

Back Cover Blurb: Greg Longenecker

Photos: William Scott Galasso

To Vicki, wife, friend and partner on our life's journey, love and gratitude.
In addition, I thank her for her cover painting and technical assistance.

I would also like to thank Greg Longenecker, for his cover notes. Susie Schaefer of Finish the Book Publishing for technical assistance and Deanna Estes of Lotus Design for the cover design.

Finally, I would like to thank members past and present of Haiku Northwest, the Southern California Haiku Study group, Haiku San Diego and Haiku North America for their invaluable workshop critiques. They have helped make this book what it is. To each and every one, my sincere gratitude.

Rough Cut
Thirty Years of Senryu

SENRYU – Haiku Society of America

Definition: A senryu is a poem, structurally similar to haiku, that highlights the foibles of human nature, usually in a humorous or satiric way.

A senryu may or may not contain a season word or a grammatical break. Some Japanese senryu seem more like aphorisms, and some modern senryu in both Japanese and English avoid humor, becoming more like serious short poems in haiku form. There are also "borderline haiku/senryu", which may seem like one or the other, depending on how the reader interprets them.

Introduction

Rough Cut is the second book in the legacy series and it consists of senryu written over the last thirty years. The first book in the series *Mixed Bag: A Travelogue in Four Forms*, focused on haiku sequences, haibun, tanka and short free verse poems. Those poems were essentially inspired by places where I lived, worked and traveled. The poems in this edition exclusively focus on human relationships and interaction. They are informed by nature as are haiku but the basis for their existence explores how we humans perceive who and what we are at our best or occasionally at our worst.

The title is meant to suggest that as human beings we are not perfect but works in progress, intellectually, emotionally and spiritually. My hope is that you may recognize your own dramatis personae among the senryu you find here or that you may connect with those you have touched or been touched by on this life's journey.

high school flame
held to my heart

her baby sleeps

cheap imitation
wanted: a life of your own
one more Elvis clone

eyeing the tote board
the T.V. evangelist
promising miracles

a fallen drunk
damning the sky
brings rain

November rain
the movie poster
ingenue in tears

        heading for work
right on cue
raindrops

        his T-shirt says
        Carpe Diem
        loudly he snores

workday
clock hands
crawling

        recession—
        dressing for work
        I tighten my belt

rest now
the workday's done,
the nightingale sings

composing haiku
rock garden perfection
teaching humility

searching
for the perfect word,
cold tea

my life in letters
the koi fanning water
small fish in a big pond

      wordless poem...
      how could you read this
      if that were true

willow's shade
the painter with her brush,
the poet with his pen

      the narcissist
      practicing scales
      memememe

blues man's song
as if he lived
every note

radio show
how odd the sound
of my own voice

raw wind
a torch song spills
out of the bar

blues man's growl...
in a roomful of mirrors
every head nods

alone in the house
all day long the riffle
of turning pages

       long ago
       the last time I saw you...
       and far away

old town clock
stops running...
no one to fix it

quite the duet
snoring puppy,
snoring wife

Friday—
the cell phones busy
with weekend plans

longest minute
counting the dial tones
before your voice

side by side...
three women all talking
on cell phones

April showers
her first time in stilettos
the earth moves again

    believe me
    she tells the friend
    who doesn't

she speaks of her ex
the pungent scent
of pepper trees

    menopause
    dueling
    thermostats

road trip
her embrace lingers,
her eyes grow moist

tail lights
the way she said
goodbye

a few precious steps...
the muscle memory
of dancehall days

road trip...
the note I thought to leave
but didn't

tuba player,
his metallic flatulence
amusing the crowd

    beret askew, a man
    plays his concertina
    as the pigeons coo

how soothing the sound
of the bamboo flute playing
in the bamboo grove

    oldies station
    talkin' bout my
    gggeneration

on Brooklyn Bridge,
the cornet player
serenades the stars

fingernail moon
on a summer evening
    cool jazz

festival of rhythm—
drummers' hands urge
dancing feet

his fingers reading
the Braille of strings
blind guitar player

mom's letters...
all the childhood memories
well up in my eyes

her voice
in my tired mind
...sleep

    when Mom sang
    even the birds
    stopped to listen

    Easter egg hunt
    Grandma's hint where
    the purple egg lies

in flagrante delicto
licking the sauce spoon
dad's eyes narrow

       out of his mouth,
       his father's words

a child aping
his father's frown
elicits a grin

my father's anger—
approaching the purple
of ripened plums

late season figs
my father's face
as he tasted them

snowball fight...
on the same side for once
Dad and I

DNA test
 the past we never
 talked about

        Lent
         giving up smoke
          and mirrors

in the old country
a truck bares my family name
roots passing by

little sister told
she looks like Daddy, cries
... Daddy's bald

    hoisted up on
    dad's shoulders, little girl
    with her mother's face

    baby's ears
    cupped by Daddy's hands,
    the boom of a cannon

    child asleep
    daddy still reading
      Prince Caspian

a heart beneath
an underlined paragraph
    used book

catacombs
a sense that
the time is near

home movies
the living and the dead
at play again

sky walking moon
night hawking son
late blooming day

      goodbye hug,
    through my father's jacket
        skin and bones

cursing me
with his last words,
my father

father says goodbye
packed away in boxes
the youth I'm leaving

       so angry the voice
       I hardly recognize it
       as my father's

father's ring---
the ties that
bind us still

family heirlooms...
let the games
begin

death certificate
before the ink dries
squabbles

in the graveyard
fireflies blink on,
blink off

I'll miss the lark song
in the morning, she said...
then closed her eyes

full mailbox...
the birthday wishes
she'll never receive

chanting...
in the pause to inhale,
a sense of death

family photos—
to what exile has
this child fled

        knots in the hair
        of a weeping girl, head
        buried in her hands

photos
not of my friends
but their children

learning to sign...
now she can cuss
with her fingers

mute, signing thanks
with dancing fingers
and a smile

the deaf actress
drinking sight and scent
signs beautiful

mime's hands
sweep high and low
walls closing in

tapping a white cane
cracks in the pavement
hiding bad luck

red star stamp
on my upturned wrist
...blues again

he blames her
for hurting his hand
on her jaw

in a shop window
the glare of an old sourpuss
walking beside me

broken truce...
ambulance sirens
puncture the night

Broadway at dusk
rain and neon glaze
the city's streets

apartment dwellers
imprisoned
by T.V. jailers

      Dawn
      the surf break sound
      of distant traffic

           spray painted
           in black and white,
           state of the nation

skyscrapers
the ant that is me
beneath them

t
h
i   c
r   r
t   a
e   n
e   e
n   s
the city skyline
readjusts

gray afternoon
stuttering traffic
all the tired faces

pick-up game
the many hues of
shirts and skins

once upon a time
the friendly skies

matinee...
one of us
still hungry

a hole in the sky
patched by drifting clouds
still the melanoma

      fog...
      everything I thought
      I knew

chemotherapy...
a mile-long strip
of roadside poppies

the kiss
that's not a kiss
flu season

      chest pains
      ...not the heart
      full moon, brighter

   flutter of eyelids
   her long journey back
     begins

roadside poppies
one more pill
to dull the pain

cliff edge...

why this sudden urge

to fly

no prison cell
no cage of bones
...free at last

(for Johnny Baranski)

March visit
with old friends...
little did we know

      obituary...
      the name of a woman
      I loved as a girl

funeral
for an old hippie
no one wears black

widower
through a window
pixilated by rain

speak to me of joy...
in her passing I have
forgotten it

one-year widow
she sleeps in his shirt
for the last time

in the limousine
between two blondes,
the heat of their hips

        blond wearing a tan
        her tiny suit says "Guess"
        ...I don't have to

summer cocktail...
her secret ingredient
passionfruit

nude sunbather,
an amateur paparazzi
spoils her solitude

skinny dip
the taste of salt
on her ear lobe

she zigs
he zags
mating season

separated by
a common language
his and hers

love scene—
he and she forget
they're acting

peccadillo
it's not me you love,
just the words I use

comb over
another white lie...
among many

two birthdays
a day apart
old lovers

she smiles…light's out
in a crescent moon's cusp
Venus ascending

the redness
of the wine on
her parted lips

two pairs of eyes
and two pairs of hands
speaking the unspoken

removing her blouse
she asks what I'd like
for my birthday

peach in hand,
I contemplate the fullness
of her figure

    fresh paint
    on the picket fence,
    newlyweds

    fruit vendor
    for her he picks
    a perfect peach

as our lips meet...
me in her eyes,
she in mine

her dance
tightening
my jeans

the time it takes
to undo buttons
lovers in stitches

rising heat
through my cotton
your silk

morning dew
on the tip of my tongue
you

she makes a joyful noise
and the making of it
makes my day

her orgasm
shivers me
into mine

after...
even our breathing
slows in tune

changing tide...
between moon and sea
between you and me

        tide in, tide out
        ashes
        on the ocean

riptide
her fear of drowning
in someone else

        hurricanes
        with male names
        adjusting

wondering why it is
that lovers always kiss
with their eyes closed

cold hands slipping
under a warm sweater,
the shock of our skins

waking...
her head on my heart,
her hand further South

moment of release—
four taut legs and
twenty toes curling

        with her eyes, asking
        where I'm going
        without her

coming home late,
as I approach the bed
one eye opens

guilt
silent apologies
toss and turn

she is using
the tone of voice I'd hate
...if I could hear it

Sierra switchbacks...
she loves me not,
she loves me

sting of a wasp
...reading her letter
stung twice

argument over
the fly on the wall
takes wing

rattle of hail
her phone voice
becoming shrill

her tone of voice...
one hundred degrees
in the shade

thunderstorm
was it something I said
or merely thought

discussion over,
we sit with regret and
cold tea between us

        Easter Sunday
        her hand clasps mine
        ...resurrection

road trip
her embrace lingers,
her eyes grow moist

        crossroads...
        get home or
        get gone

moving on
the surf break sound
of distant traffic

leaves cast adrift
my past imperfect
yours too

gift exchange...
forget-me-nots,
belladonna

let it not touch us...
the wind which tears
these clouds apart

talking divorce...
the yowling of a tomcat
in the vacant lot

make up sex
sometimes
it works

offkey
the warbler's song
...divorce papers

post-divorce
the fatherless photos
of children

the door closes...
something permanent
in the click of its bolt

tail lights
the way she said
goodbye

yesterday's song
old wounds
reopened

tampons
in the medicine cabinet
she stays late

a word
I rarely apply to women
in *this* case fits

burning sheets
the words
we can't take back

evening rain
the breeze cools
these lovers' sheets

dragon dancing
on his tattooed arm
her fingers impressed

the cost of cool
sting of red wine
on pierced lip

another's name
on his tattooed arm
her nails draw blood

hardening
on my tongue
her nipples

arising when
her curvature meets
my perpendicular

a sudden stiffness
awakens me,
her mischievous grin

invited

I enter
her aura

      inside
      surrounded by you
      me

still...
in my yawning mouth
the taste of her

the baby's fingers
trace my middle-aged face,
unravel a smile

conjoined twins—
after the operation
two children, alone

baby's fist
not letting go
of my pinkie

childproof cap
only the five-year old
can open it

singing a song
she just made up,
girl on a swing

old hippies' pond,
stocked with trout
and a laughing Buddha

latest disguise
an old man feeding
pigeons in the park

empty house—
the kitchen wall calendar
thirty years old

above and below
all around: in my face
in my heart...gray

awakened—
a cat's paw
strokes my beard

bucket list...
my nephew asks
what's on mine

cycling past
the graveyard...
stopped watch

    passing through   *and I*
just   *the clouds*

morning...
a canoe
adrift

photo album,
loved ones lost
alive again

gooseflesh...
a shadow crosses
the shuttered room

whispers...
when I turn the light on,
nobody there

mother's eyes
in father's face...
his own strong lungs

silence so perfect,
I don't even
talk to myself

Ash Wednesday—
the sins of the father
that can't be seen

moonlight on cabins
of the old slave street
low moan of wind

fireflies
in the wheat field
...Gettysburg

Andersonville...
under Georgia's red earth
so many "unknowns"

Mid-day heat—
hawks above Rosebud River
circling the dead

horseshoe crab...
on another sixth of June
helmets in the sand

not wanting to know
rats
in war zone rubble

two front war
Red Tails*
go for broke+

*Tuskegee Airmen
+ motto of Japanese-American
442nd regimental combat team

at the sound
of collapsing towers
pigeons take flight

        shining on the names
        of long dead heroes
        winter sun

where twin towers stood...
the emptiness of sky
and missing persons

another shooting
the flag at half-staff staff
semi-permanent

border town
neighborhood children play
red light, green light

hunting
for the exit door
just in case

rumors of war
in the family room...
a smoke on the porch

drumbeats and
the sound of marching feet
again

before
the tripwire
after

squawking hens,
strutting roosters...
senate hearings

blood moon
the newscaster's rhetoric
heats up

seeds of hatred
once sown
harvest white crosses

joysticks...
the rising sound of
drums and drones

Thanksgiving—
reading the "Dear John" letter
again and again

   oil addiction
a father's life stolen
from his newborn

Christmas Eve...
in her bed, in his foxhole
dreaming each other

Christmas dinner
mid-east fears
eyes on the empty chair

Mrs. Claus
underneath her red robe
my Christmas present

    Christmas list
    every year
    shorter

parting the lovers
never apart
a sniper's bullets

blast victim...
in a blackened hand
a fig half-eaten

amputee vet...
gone are the hands she loved
to have touch her

west wind
unfurling the flag,
a tearing sound

bomb blast—
peace proposal headlines,
splattered with blood

collateral damage
words liberators apply
to dead children

moonscape
the pocked playground
of Aleppo's children

Memorial Day
with each new flag
sorrows multiply

one year ago
eyes on the empty chair
tears, still empty

Memorial Day...
beside cross, crescent, star
same flag

Memorial Day—
her husband's name in granite
all that she can touch

        cracked bell
        liberty's light
        shines through

Memorial Day...
more heroes to remember,
more flags each year

        state of the nation
        spray painted
        in black and white

bottle
broken as the life
beside it

to the well
once too often
...wine stains

homeless man
exchanging a scarecrow's shirt
for his own

expletives...
the town drunk chafes
when coyote howls

homeless man
wearing Santa's red hat,
no toys in that bag

      clean coin pressed
      into filthy hands
      poor homeless man

      homeless man
      berating the wind and
      someone unseen

lottery ticket
in a homeless man's hand
what are the odds

orphaned pets
family reunions,
no words and yet

woolen blankets
Gore-Tex coats...
not forgotten

hot coffee
a new pair of gloves
baristas gift

limo driver
hands out Benjamins+
source unknown

+ $100 US

bitter wind
on a bus station bench
anonymous

tattered shawl
yet she bends to feed
the feral cat

hot soup passed
into cold hands...
the shadow of her smile

after a meal, shower
and shave, the hobo
who looks like us

fog lifts
the first full day
of sobriety

minimum wage
she sleeps in her car
this winter night

unremarkable
woman walking towards me
then she smiles

in mid-sentence
her eyes leave mine,
old flame

her body language,
offering more than
casual conversation

        lava flow...
        the heat as you
        stand beside me

found penny--
a patina of rust
on my birth year

bachelor party...
to wear or not to wear
the wedding ring

grinding my teeth...
if I had them, I could
find them, lost glasses

movie night
senior discount please
why not, I earned it

long lost brother calls...
our brief conversation
still all about him

torrential rain...
her estranged brother's
sudden death

first meeting
of half-brothers,
the gaps we fill

family reunion
hurricane warnings
dominate the news

        favorite uncle...
        the planned visit
        becomes a funeral

whispers...
when I turn the light on,
nobody there

Father's Day —
again, he refuses
to take my call

      errant throw—
      an audible curse from
      the child's father

      Father's Day
      the question lingers...
      how much of you in me

hand-in-hand
squeeze once for Yes,
twice for No

to remove
or not to remove...
the feeding tube

shallow breaths...
where his eyes go
I can't follow

moments away
from father's dying breath
...forgiveness

memoirs—
now that he's gone I begin
to understand him

not forgetting
to forgive myself
...and you

swift wings...
myself in a dream
last night

contrails
to all the places
I will go

old flame
now she wants
to friend me

opening our wedding album
a ray of sunshine,
motes of dust

pen to paper...
my only words
today

unfortunately...
I don't bother
to read the rest

her Valentine's card
a rainbow of raised hearts
for my fingertips

      fingertips
      when words won't
      suffice

dog tags...
her fingers caress
his name

avian madrigal
in dappled woods...
I just tweet

canyon echo
my voice, thought lost
comes back

sister's solo
on certain notes
mother's voice

wind keens
through skeletal trees
the echo of your voice

      tuning in...
      what she says
      what she doesn't say

poetry reading...
on that singular phrase
a glottal stop

between hedgerows
train tracks lead
everywhere
...and nowhere

train whistle...
the conductor's mood
by its sound

like a dinosaur
snoring
fat man in a subway car

train whistle
further and further
our paths diverge

seaside bench
seven cigarette butts
decisions, decisions

Goodbye
the hardest word to say
sometimes

fire whirl...
her tongue inflamed
by accusation

sidewalk café'
her love life lousy...
now we all know

hip new bistro
when did I become
invisible

airport bar...
the twice-told tales
of strangers

Continental Divide
red states and blue
...purple passions

stranded
in the airport lobby
passengers reboot

shutters secure
what we have kindled
begins to burn

rain smacks
the hotel's awning...
separate cabs

dead
the painted vase
apology roses

low tide...
the wedding ring slips
from her finger

        email received...
        I can read the message
        but not your eyes

glacial ice
the way her blue eyes
took the news

the eyes
I used to read
shut me out

a frozen smile
on parted lips
a wooden embrace

side-by-side
hand-in-hand, yet
I miss her already

the portrait complete
what lingers is the scent
of paint

        Mt. Olympus . . .
        our 25th anniversary
        relighting the torch

the artist's painting
of her husband, now I know
what she sees in me

Anniversary dinner—
we get the same
cookie fortune

opening our wedding
album, a ray of sunshine
and motes of dust

fifty years
under the linden tree,
still holding hands

glucose test...
all the sweet things
I must give up

        silent ceremony
        we walk the spiral path

the old hermit
coming only so close
as his waving hand

closing time...
my eyes look up
to face the rain

        small circle
        where her ring was...
        closing time

closing time...
rain glazed street
and no place to go

old neighborhood
same streets
new tongues

the years I spent
on this house on the hill,
the years after

in between
the old home and the new
this heart

streaking
the gossip's window,
acid rain

numbers on his arm...
a grandchild asks
how he got them

Grandma declares
Grandpa full of whimsy...
I thought it was gas

fence line--
barbed wire
between us

two flags
straddle the razor wire
both wave

synagogue walls
citizens extract
a swastika

sporting legacy
father and son spit
watermelon seeds

father and son—
laughing as the snow
turns yellow

school assembly
the din before
the dope

texting, texting
she never saw
the truck ahead

weary   weary
until the sunset's clouds
sprout wings

texting, texting
she plows into me
says not a word

the bass hum
of bow on strings...
her deepest secret

      silent prayer
      it all comes down to
      a single word

Milky Way...
so many stars
to wish upon

fish hook moon
above the lake...
she reels me in

retired fisherman
his heart goes out
with the morning tide

retirement home
someone's grandchild
missing a sock

daybreak
in the rearview mirror
retirement home

retired
his coffee cup
still working

elderly shopper
... a fine opportunity
to practice patience

retirement
he refuses to fix
the broken watch

pussy
you can say it in public
now that it goes with hat

as if smoke
and smog were not enough
teargas

after the fire
hugs from neighbors
she never knew

twenty-fifth
high school reunion
...embers

       the one person
       I didn't want to see
       extends his hand

school reunion
have we become
our parents?

forty-fifth reunion
stretching my workout
just a little longer

gathered years
frosting my beard
but not my smile

yoga pose
stretching the old body
into the new

sunrise tai chi
footprints erased
in the chant of waves

judo master
confined to a wheel chair
still has a few moves

separated
by a common language
his and hers

the weaker sex?
tell it to the mantis
or the widow in black

pretty woman
all the sailors' eyes
at attention

naval maneuvers
a belly dancer shows
how flesh makes waves

high school flame

held to my heart
her baby sleeps

recurring dream...
I had almost forgotten
the joy of flight

potter's field...
nameless bones teaching
forgotten things

family bible
her maiden name
in (   )

one breath

the difference between

I am and I was

ACKNOWLEDGMENTS:

HNW & HSA Anthologies:
When Butterflies Come, 1993, an HSA members Anthology as are 1995 *Sudden Shower, Echoes Across the Cascades,* 1996 *Unbroken Curve,* 1997 *Sunlight Through Rain,* 1998 *Cherry Blossom Rain,* 1999, *The Swinging Grasshopper,* 2000 *To Find the Words, Wind Five-Folded* (Tanka Anthology, AHA Books), *All Day Long* (HPNC Anthology), *Geese* (Anthology) 1999, HSA Anthology 2000 *Crinkled Sunshine, Wind Shows Itself* (Haiku NW), 2004, *Tracing the Fern,* (Haiku North America anthology), 2005, HSA anthology, *Loose Change,* 2005, *Lanterns: a Firefly Anthology* 2007, *Among Water Lilies,* A White Lotus Anthology 2008, *Seed Packets:* an anthology of flower haiku, 2009, a Bottle Rockets anthology, *Sharing the Sun,* 2010 HSA anthology, In *Pine Shade,* 2011 HSA members anthology, *Standing Still,* 2011 an HNA members Anthology, *Dreams Wander On: Contemporary Poems of Death Awareness,* ed. Robert Epstein (a 2011 Anthology), *The Temple Bell Stops: Contemporary Poems*

on Grief, Loss and Change, edited by Robert Epstein (a 2012 anthology), *This World,* (a 2013 HSA Anthology), *Now This: Contemporary Poems of Beginnings, Renewals, and Firsts* (a 2013 Anthology); *A Warm Welcome,* (a 2013 Seabeck anthology); *No Longer Strangers,* (a 2014 Haiku Northwest Anthology); *Take Out Window,* HSA 2014 anthology. *The Spirit in Contemporary Haiku,* ed. by Robert Epstein 2014, *Rainsong,* (a 2014 Seabeck anthology); *Drawn to the Light,* a SCHSG Anthology, 2015, *A Splash on Water,* HSA 2015 anthology. *Fire in the Treetops,* (Celebrating Twenty-five Years of Haiku North America), 2016 HSA anthology *What the Wind Can't Touch, Every Chicken, Cow, Fish and Frog* (Animal Rights Issue), 2016 *Write Like Issa* (How-to Anthology), 2017. *Haiku Canada Review, Eclipse Moon,* 2017 SCHSG 20th Anniversary Issue, *Earthsigns,* a HNA 2017 Anthology, *On Down the Road,* HSA 2017 Anthology, *Gift of Silence: A Haiku Tribute to Leonard Cohen,* 2018, *A Sonic Boom of Stars,* a SCHSG Anthology 2019.

Haiku/Senryu Journals & Magazines:

Cicada, Red Pagoda, Modern Haiku, Brussels Sprout, Mirrors, Backyard Bamboo, Woodnotes, Tandava, Antfarm, Haiku Headlines, Frogpond, New Cicada (Japan), Lynx, Haiku Canada, New Zealand Haiku, Ko (Japan), Piedmont Literary Review, black bough, San Francisco Haiku Anthology, Bear Creek Review, Northwest Literary Forum, Point Judith Light, Haiku Northwest booklet '93, HWUP, Tight, Blithe Spirit (Essex, England), Lilliput Review, Albatross (Romania), Haiku Haven, Orphic Lute, Wheel of Dharma, Honolulu Advertiser, Spin (New Zealand). Ant, ant, ant, ant, ant, VRABAC (Sparrow) (Croatia), Haiku Quarterly (England), Hummingbird, Raw Nervz (Canada), Seaoats International, Presence (England), Tundra, Chiyo-Laughing CyPress, Silver Wings, Hokumeisha Haikukai (Japan), Paper Wasp (Australia), Heron's Nest, A Hundred Gourds (Australia). Key-ku: Haiku of the Keys (Solares Hill), Brevities, Treetops, Famous Reporter (Australia), Mariposa, White Lotus, Blackwidow's Web of Poetry, Haiku Hippodrome, Moonset, South by Southeast, HAIKU PAGE, Wisteria, Kokako (NZ), California Quarterly, Mambo (Kenya).

Online Journals & Blogs:

Simply Haiku, (Senryu section), electronic magazine, *Asian Geographic Magazine (the Read),* (Singapore), *Cattails* (online journal-Haiku Oregon), *Four and Twenty,* (online journal), *Kernals, Sonic Boom,* (India), *Frozen Butterfly,* (Austria) *Prune Juice, FAILED HAIKU, Autumn Moon Haiku Journal, Under the Basho* (India), *The Bamboo Hut, Otata* (AU), Annual H. Gene Murtha Memorial Senryu Contest/Prune Juice.

REVIEWS OF PREVIOUS BOOKS

Summer's Early Light (1973)
Phoenix: Songs of the Firebird (1981)
Cascadia and Emerald Rain (1993)
Vermilion Falling (1994) [sold out]

Mini-reviews:

for *Rainbow Music:* "If you don't plan to buy another small press contribution for the remainder of the year indulge yourself..." - Joyce Carbone, *Cerebus*

for *Full Moon Serenade:* "Galasso's sense perceptions are vibrating with song...this book of poetry is a gift to the reader."
- Marjorie Buettner, *Modern Haiku*

for *Blood (family and Ink):* "Combined with candor, perception and interesting approaches, both simple and complex subjects are made interesting...some real gems."
- Martin Latter, *Peace and Freedom* (U.K)

for *Odori, Blue:* "His poems are crisp, and honest, written with a deft touch that is uniquely beautiful." – Carrie Ann Thunnel, *White Lotus/Nisqually Delta Review*

for *Laughing Out Clouds*: "I'll never forget reading this collection ...beautiful, insightful and uplifting poetry resonates with any reader with a soul." – Paul Rance (ed. *Peace and Freedom* (U.K)

for *Sea, Mist and Sitka Spruce:* "Another collection by the very prolific William Scott Galasso in a wide variety of journals I particularly enjoyed the autumn and winter images..." - Moira Richards, Book editor, South Africa

for *Collage:* "Scott Galasso's latest collection is one of the best books of poetry that I have read... This is the truth is what we want and don't get elsewhere. This is writing that we trust, a remarkable collection." - J. Glenn Evans, Founder of Poetswest, author of *Window in the Sky, Buffalo Tracks* and this from Christopher Jarmick, author of *The Glass Cocoon* and *Ignition: Poem Starters, Septuplets, Statements and Double Dog Dares* "Encompassing some of his best work from 1973 to 2012 is ambitious, humorous, compassionate and as honest and nakedly human as anything you're likely to read."

For additional information or copies of these books email:

galwinpress@yahoo.com

Note: The latter two books are available on Amazon for $10.00.

for *Silver Salmon Runes:* "I get a sense of authenticity and integrity as if I were reading someone's journal." - Randy Brooks, *Mayfly*

and this from Marjorie Buettner, *Modern Haiku:* "Keen observations that do what good haiku do: provide a unique viewpoint on the ordinary world."

for *Mixed Bag: A Travelogue in Four Forms*

"...Plenty of haibun and haiku stick in the mind like postcards worthy of a prominent place on a corkboard or refrigerator door. Yet though we travel the world, someplace in the heart remain mutely mysterious, *nothing to say/only my hands and arms/can speak.* "

   Eds., *Modern Haiku*

And this from Dave Read, *Haiku Canada* davereadpoetry.blogspot.ca

"Galasso is a talented and unique writer.... Mixed Bag is a good book of poetry that takes us through Galasso's many travels, experiences, and philosophies. Galasso effectively makes use of haibun, haiku sequences, short free verse poems, and tanka to showcase his world of adventure."

PREVIEWS - COMING SOON!
Orphans **(Poems 2012-2019)**

ALEPH

> The Aleph was about two to three centimeters in diameter, but all of cosmic space was there, with no diminution in size. Each thing was infinite, because I could clearly see it from every point on the universe.
>
> -- Jorge Luis Borges, The Aleph

The dead star's light still illuminates night. The moment that was, is and will be connected, Time bats an eye. The first kiss warm on the lips meets the last breath escaping the body. Past lives, future visions collapse in the moment. I stand by the sea as the tides change, as I stand on the mountain, snow at my feet, as I stand before a stele in Rome or feel the dew of Erin's grass wet between my toes. My mother's blood flows through my body, my father's lungs pump air in and out.

I am a babe in arms, a child on the verge of language, a man strong in his prime, a weathered elder, at what instant does one become another?

We are dancers in a cosmic circle, attuned to spherical music and those we loved remain with us, the space dust of cells in a soul.

My sincerest thanks and appreciation to Gregory Longenecker for writing the back cover. Greg is a two-time winner of the H. Gene Murtha Senryu Contest, and author of *Somewhere Inside Yesterday*, whose title haiku was short-listed for a Touchstone Award. He was a featured poet in *A New Resonance 9*, editor for the Southern California Haiku Study Group's Members' Anthology and has given talks on his haiku and haiku topics for Haiku North America, Haiku Poets' of Northern California, SCHSG, San Diego Haiku Society and the Yuki Teikei Haiku Society. Gregory has twice chaired the YTHS Tokutomi Haiku Contest and also been a judge for the Haiku Society of America's Haibun Contest.

www.ingramcontent.com/pod-product-compliance
Lightning Source LLC
Chambersburg PA
CBHW051345040426
42453CB00007B/414